OF
OM

**A NEW SPIRIT FOR
A NEW MILLENNIUM**

Jatinder Singh

Published by Jatinder Singh
PO Box 1545, Slough, Berks, SL1 2GS, UK.
Jindi@hotmail.com

First published by Jatinder Singh, 2000
Printed by CSJS Exports, Amritsar, India, 143001.

Copyright © Jatinder Singh, 2000
All rights reserved

This book is sold subject to the condition that it shall not, by way of trade or otherwise, be lent, re-sold, hired out, or otherwise circulated without the publisher's prior consent in any form of binding or cover other than that in which it is published and without a similar condition including this condition being imposed on the subsequent purchaser

THE LITTLE BOOK OF
SPIRITUAL WISDOM

The little book of spiritual wisdom is written for the seeker in today's modern world. At a time when old forms of thinking are passing away from our every day lives, new spiritual wisdom is sought by many.

These teachings, based on several Sikh writings, span nearly a thousand years of spiritual wisdom, exploring the oneness of experience for seekers throughout history.

This little book will be of immense appeal to today's genuine seeker. These wisdoms remain little-known to the world, a hidden treasure waiting to be explored. These truths illuminate the heart of the human condition and explore the central issues of human experience, allowing the seeker to explore hidden treasures and secrets within themselves.

This book is not intended to be full of spiritual riddles, but straight to the point for every seeker. No vast knowledge is needed to understand the truths in these teachings. You will find these wisdoms relevant in your every day life. It is my sincere hope that these teachings enrich the lives of those who read, get inspired and act upon them.

                                      Jatinder Singh

ALIKE

They for whom praise and abuse are alike,
for whom iron and gold are alike ...
know that they are truly free.

Guru Tegh Bahadur
1621-1675

Take the good with the bad. If you do not get overly proud because of praise or overly unhappy from criticism, then you have understood how to manage the mind. This way, you will avoid anguish and continually feel solace.

AWAKE

Awake is the life of those who know love.
Say goodbye, O Goya, to the dawn of sleep.

Bhai Nand Lal
1633-1713

Love is spirituality. Only through sincere love can you fully experience the various realms and states of spirituality.

For the religious, this means sincere love for God and God's creation. This love for God is the essence of all faith.

BODY AND SOUL

*The body is the tree,
the bird of the soul dwells within it.*

Guru Amar Das
1479-1574

The soul is not tied to the body. Once death approaches, it is only the body that meets its end. At this time, like a bird, the soul will take flight to continue its journey.

The CHASE

*The natural tendency of the mind
is to chase the mind.*

Bhagat Kabir
1398-1448

The mind is forever chasing itself. Make it your first task to slow down and take a break. Contemplation and relaxation will give the answers to the questions of your runaway mind.

The DEER

*The deer does not know the secret;
the musk is within its own body,
but it searches for it outside.*

Bhagat Ravidas
15th Century

Like a deer, we often search for answers outside ourselves. We cover lands, visit many places and people, looking for the answer to the soul's anguish. The true seeker realises that the answers lie within. Before trying to solve some spiritual problem, contemplate on the good inside you. It will point you towards the solution.

DIVINE LIGHT

*Whoever does the deeds of the soul,
day and night,
sees the immaculate Divine Light deep within.*

Guru Nanak Dev
1469-1539

Even those who do not have belief in religion still recognise the power of the soul. Take time out to meet the needs of the soul and you will eventually begin to feel the glow of divine light within yourself.

DREAM

*Like the king, asleep upon his throne
dreaming that he is a beggar ...
Such is my own condition.*

Bhagat Ravidas
15th Century

You are precious. We are all kings and queens in our own right. Every human being is precious. Do not walk around in a dream-like state, not realising your true wealth.

EFFORT

*Through sincere efforts,
the mind is made peaceful and calm.*

Guru Arjun Dev
1563-1606

Only sincere effort brings results. No clever tricks can bring calm and peace to the mind and strengthen the soul. Only through sincere worship can your spirituality flourish within.

EGOTISM

Egotism and possessiveness are very enticing; egotistical pride has plundered everyone.

Guru Nanak Dev
1469 - 1539

Egotism is one of the biggest obstacles in achieving a state of spiritual bliss. Those who forever think and say 'I, I' can never appreciate what they have or respect the feelings and ways of other people. Stop your ego; think of others, have love in your heart and meditate as often as possible.

EXCELLENT LIFE

*Practice truth, contentment and kindness;
this is the most excellent way of life.*

Guru Arjun Dev
1563-1606

The simplest things make for the best life. Seeking simple qualities will transform you forever. Think about the truth, feel content with what you have and keep kindness for all in your heart. It is so simple and, yet, you will find that these three qualities will lift your spirits.

FAITH

*None is faithless,
if they have faith in themselves.*

Bhai Nand Lal
1633-1713

Organised religion is fading from many lives. As a result of this, many lack some sort of faith. This is a shame. The first step towards faith is to have faith in yourself. This is the stepping stone to realising true faith, peace and contentment. Believe in yourself. A lack of self-conviction can only lead to inner frustration.

FALSE

*Those who have one thing in their heart,
and something else in their mouth,
are judged to be false.*

Sheikh Farid
1173-1265

Always say what you mean and know to be true. Avoid making up stories in order to impress someone or to avoid some difficult circumstance. The truth will ultimately prevail. No one likes someone who is false. Present the real you to everyone you meet. They will both appreciate and like the real you.

FEAR

Fear no one and give fear to no one.

Guru Tegh Bahadur
1621-1675

Fear is good for no one and a very destructive feeling. Try not to feel afraid of anything and remember never to put fear into others. This way, fear will not grip and burden your life.

FLOWER

*If one obtains the subtle fragrance
of that spiritual flower,
he cannot describe the indescribable;
he could speak, but who would understand?*

Bhagat Kabir
1398-1448

Spiritual experience is beyond description. Like the smell of a beautiful flower, spiritual experience cannot be fully described by the one who experiences it. One thing is for sure; spiritual and mystical experiences are life-changers.

FORGIVENESS

*To practice forgiveness
is the true fast, good conduct and contentment.*

Guru Arjun Dev
1563-1606

It can be very hard to forgive. However, if you do, then others will see the good in you and your own grief over being hurt by someone else will not dig into you. It is far better to forgive and move on.

GIVE

*One gets hereafter
only what one gives here
out of honest earnings.*

Guru Nanak Dev
1469-1539

To give is divine. As you give and foster love for others now, so your soul shall receive the rewards on its journey after this life.

GOOD AND BAD

*From the One Light,
the entire universe welled up.
So who is good, and who is bad?*

Bhagat Kabir
1398-1448

How can we call anyone good or bad? One divine light pervades and creates us all. Realise this and you would have grasped one of the most important spiritual truths realised by saints through the ages.

GOOD CONDUCT

If you seek the path of good conduct, forsake greed, and do not look upon another's property and women.

Bhagat Jaidev
12th Century

Good conduct will never go out of fashion. Avoid materialism and envy and act in a way such that peace and contentment surround each and every act you perform.

GOSSIP

*One whose heart is filled with malicious gossip
... everything he does is in vain.*

Guru Ram Das
1534-1581

Everyone enjoys a good gossip, but no one wants others to gossip about them. Gossip only brings negativity. Avoid gossip and accept that everyone, just like yourself, has ups and downs in their lives.

GREED

*When there is greed, what love can there be?
When there is greed, love is false.
How long can one remain in a thatched hut
which leaks when it rains?*

Sheikh Farid
1173-1265

Replace greed with love. Do not allow your mind to be filled with greed. It can be difficult to feel content, but sincere effort will allow you to overcome greed. Take steps to stop the feeling of greed by nurturing love in your heart.

HARSH WORDS

Harsh words bring only grief.

Guru Nanak Dev
1469-1539

In our anger, we can say many bitter words. In that moment of frustration this aggressive behaviour brings you relief, but in the long run the guilt and realisation of your harsh words will only bring you sorrow. It is best to think before you speak. It is better not to speak, if it only brings negativity to the conversation.

HARVEST

As you plant, so shall you reap.

Guru Nanak Dev
1469-1539

The seeds of positive thought and action will be enjoyed when they flourish. Begin to do good and positive things for yourself now. It will bring you more happiness and foster good character for the future.

HUMANITY

Recognise the whole human race as one.

Guru Gobind Singh
1666-1708

Living in a big world, we constantly meet people from different backgrounds. With these different paths continually crossing yours, it is important to remember that we are all human beings.

HUMILITY

*The fruit of humility is
intuitive peace and pleasure.*

Guru Arjun Dev
1563-1606

The humble character will never feel frustration. It is important to set goals in life, but these needn't be materialistic ones. Try humility for a week and see how your inner self glows and feels free from self-made pressures.

JEALOUSY

*I have given up jealousy,
ever since I associated
with the company of saints.*

Guru Arjun Dev
1563-1606

Jealousy can eat away at you. It is difficult not to feel jealous about another's fortune. If you feel jealousy creeping into your mind, then try to think of someone good, peaceful and content and think of how they would deal with this feeling. Be happy for the fortunes of others as your time of good fortune will eventually come.

JEWEL

Deep within the nucleus of the self is the jewel.

Guru Amar Das
1479-1574

The treasures we look for outside, are within ourselves. You are precious. Realise your wealth and enjoy the depth of your own spirituality. You only need to meditate on the pure love that is within you to begin to realise what this jewel is.

KNOWLEDGE

*Knowledge grows in the seeker,
it's light fades in those who argue.*

Guru Nanak Dev
1469-1539

Arguing prevents you from learning. Discussion and openness allows you to develop as a person. Arguing your point across to others means you never learn anything new yourself. If you seek new ideas and thoughts, then your knowledge will grow.

LIGHT IN ALL

*Forget caste,
recognise the one light in all.*

Guru Nanak Dev
1469-1539

Divisions are man-made. Do not waste time believing in any ideals that promote differentiation between people. We are all human beings with the same universal divine light illuminating our souls.

LIVING

*Truth is high,
higher still is truthful living.*

Guru Nanak Dev
1469-1539

Live the truth. The highest state of spirituality is only accessed once you begin to live your own life truthfully.

LOTUS HEART

*When the intellect achieves spiritual wisdom,
the lotus heart blossoms forth.*

Guru Amar Das
1479-1574

Spiritual wisdom is the most important thing to gain. This is the only wisdom that can answer the issues of the heart. Once you begin to develop an understanding of the spiritual you, then your heart will begin to blossom like a lotus, opening and leading you to new horizons.

MARRIAGE

*They are not said to be husband and wife,
who merely sit together.
They alone are called husband and wife,
who have one light in two bodies.*

Guru Amar Das
1479-1574

Marriage is not a mere contract between two people but a meeting of two souls. True marriage lies in the harmony of the couple's physical and spiritual worlds.

MIND

*Win over your mind,
and you shall win over the world.*

Guru Nanak Dev
1469-1539

At times, our mind can be our worst enemy. If you can control the pressures of your mind, then the outside world will become more manageable.

ONE BREATH

*There is only one breath,
we are all made of the same clay.*

Guru Ram Das
1534-1581

We all breathe the same air. We share this planet. We are all made from the same elements. Remember this when your mind begins to differentiate between people.

POWER

*I respectively bow to those who have power,
yet remain humble.*

Bhai Gurdas
1551-1636

Power can destroy or heal. Power can turn the mind away from the needs of the soul. Those people who have power, yet attend to the needs of their spirit, realise what true power is. When you have power always remember your humility towards others.

QUARREL

*Do not fall into a quarrel
by calling someone bad.*

Guru Nanak Dev
1469-1539

Quarrels bring grief to all those involved. No quarrel can solve a problem. Avoid such negativity and look for a positive solution to every situation you face.

RACE

We all have the same eyes, ears, body and figure, made out of earth, air, fire and water.

Guru Gobind Singh
1666-1708

Discrimination is ignorance. It breeds on our lack of knowledge of other people's cultures and ways. One fact we can all bare in mind is that we are all human beings with the same physical features and created in the same way. This simplistic fact can begin to cure discrimination that rests in our minds.

The SWAN

*Saintly people continually peck
at the Divine Name,
like swans pecking at pearls in the ocean.*

Guru Amar Das
1479-1574

The company of saintly and good people is sought by all. Seek the company of those who make you feel happy, comfortable and peaceful. Soon, you will find that you become like them and enrich your own daily feelings and experiences.

SECRET WITHIN

*Deep within the self is the secret,
but the fool looks for it outside.*

Guru Amar Das
1479-1574

There is a secret within us all. Many people search outside for those things that will answer their soul's questions. However, contemplating on the innermost you and through sincere effort, you will find that all the answers to your questions are found within you.

The SELF

*Those who recognise the self,
their minds become pure.*

Guru Amar Das
1479-1574

Those who do not recognise their inner-selves are continually fraught with anxiety. Understand and respect who you are. Only through self-recognition can peace come within your being.

SELF-RESPECT

*If one lives without self-respect,
all that one eats goes to waste.*

Guru Nanak Dev
1469-1539

Respect yourself. Once you can appreciate your self worth, then you can begin to respect and understand your surroundings.

SERVICE

*Through selfless service,
eternal peace is obtained.*

Guru Amar Das
1479-1574

Voluntary service helps both the giver and needy. Taking some time out to help others on their life journey ultimately helps yours. To know that you can help and comfort others, makes you realise the importance and depth of your own life.

SHOP

This body is the jeweller's shop.

Guru Nanak Dev
1469-1539

This body contains many jewels. If you search deep within yourself, through sincere effort, you will realise that there are many spiritual jewels within you. Start shopping for these jewels now!

SING AND LISTEN

Sing, and listen … Your pain shall be sent far away and peace shall come to your home.

Guru Nanak Dev
1469-1539

Singing and listening to inspirational words brings peace and contentment. Steal a few moments for faith and you will find that this makes you a greater person.

SLANDER

Slandering others amounts to putting filth into one's own mouth.

Guru Nanak Dev
1469-1539

Slander can never lead to good. Simply avoid denigrating others. Accept the good and bad in everyone.

SOUL

*The body shall turn to dust,
and the soul shall fly away.*

Guru Nanak Dev
1469-1539

The soul never dies. The body is finite, but the soul is connected to the infinite. As such, do not fear physical death as it merely indicates a new chapter in your soul's journey.

SPEECH

Tender speech fosters the bond of love.

Guru Nanak Dev
1469-1539

No one wants to listen to a bad-tempered person. Always speak gently with others. You will notice how receptive people will become to your points of view if your words are tender and kind.

STATUS

None is high, none is low.

Guru Nanak Dev
1469-1539

How do you define high and low people? People are classed by their status, wealth, background and even gender. These are man-made classifications. Someone who is high in one person's view, may be low in another's. Look upon all as equals to yourself and realise that we are all human beings.

The STREAM

*The stream of immaculate purity flows
through the home of the self within;
one who drinks from it, finds peace.*

Guru Ram Das
1534-1581

There is a light of positive power which, like a stream, surges through us all. If you can find the pure you, then bathe in that purity to feel rejuvenated.

SUPERSTITION

Get rid of your doubts and superstitions.

Guru Ram Das
1534-1581

Superstition is merely an extension of one's own insecurities. Do not look for answers in superstitious stories or rituals. These will only increase your own dependence in these false ideals. Realise the importance of your self-being and learn to take the good with the bad.

SWEETNESS

*Sweetness and humility
are the essence of all virtues.*

Guru Nanak Dev
1469-1539

Sweetness is not a complicated trait. Practise being sweet and humble to others, and see how they react to you.

TRADER

Let us be traders in the business of Truth.
This product will take us to the True Court.

Guru Arjun Dev
1563-1606

What is the best business? Which business gives the greatest wealth? What trade gives the just rewards? Truth. Trade in this and you will receive indescribable rewards.

TREE

At night, lots of birds settle on the tree.
Some are happy, some are sad.
Caught in the desires of the mind, they perish.
And when the life-night comes to its end,
they look to the sky.
They fly away in all ten directions,
according to their pre-ordained destiny.

Guru Nanak Dev
1469-1539

We live in a planet of many souls. Like birds on a tree, we will fly into the vast and limitless sky, to continue our spiritual journey. Control the whims of the mind and allow your soul to feel this freedom now.

TRUTH

*Peace and happiness shall fill
your mind deep within,
if you act according to truth and self-discipline.*

Guru Amar Das
1479-1574

All trust the truthful person. Do not get into the rut of lying and fibbing all the time. Be truthful about who you are and live with the truth of every day life. This self-discipline will allow you to expand your mind into new realms.

UNDERSTANDING

*To act without understanding
is to lose the treasure of this human life.*

Guru Amar Das
1479-1574

Reassurance comes with understanding. If you act without full understanding, then the outcome of your actions may not be to your liking. Accept and learn about each and every new circumstance and experience you face in your day to day life.

VIRTUE

*Without virtue,
this human life passes away in vain.*

Guru Nanak Dev
1469-1539

Personality goes a long way. If you have a good character, then you will enjoy the hidden treasures of life and others will find you to be a joy to be around.

WHAT IS REAL?

*The real is where
the sayable and unsayable meet.
What true reality is,
is altogether beyond comprehension.*

Bhagat Kabir
1398-1448

The world around us is describable through words. On the other hand, there are things for which no description gives justice. Between these two realms lies true reality, which is beyond comprehension but experienced by the true seeker.

ZEAL OF THE PILGRIM

*There were no signposts on the pilgrim's way,
through heaven or earth.
It was the zeal of my quest
which brought me to the threshold of worship.*

Bhai Nand Lal
1633-1713

The only rule for obtaining spirituality and self-realisation is personal effort and zeal. This zeal will lead you to the answers, as long as your quest is real and sincere.

If you have any comments or suggestions, please write to:

Jatinder Singh,
PO Box 1545,
Slough, Berks,
SL1 2GS,
U.K.

E-mail: Jindi@hotmail.com

Thank you.